LOVE YOUR BODY

THE IMPERFECT GIRL'S GUIDE TO
POSITIVE BODY IMAGE

ELIZABETH WALLING

PRAISE FOR *LOVE YOUR BODY*

"So often we think focusing on our flaws doesn't hurt anyone... some may even argue that it's what motivates them. But Elizabeth makes a compelling case that body hate, body shaming, and not loving our bodies hurts us and those around us. I wish everyone could get their hands on this book."

✳ from Robin Konie of thankyourbody.com

"As someone who lives and works in Hollywood this is a topic that I see a dire need to address daily. I'm so glad to now have an excellent resource to refer people to. Drop the magazines at the checkout stand and pick up this book instead. Elizabeth's book is part reality check, part body love manual, and part pep talk. I don't know about you but I often need a dose of all three of those things. Thank you Elizabeth for reminding us to stop nitpicking and start living our lives!"

✳ from Sylvie McCracken of hollywoodhomestead.com

"What an absolutely LOVELY book, and a message that so many of us women need to hear. Negative body image can steal the fun, love and experiences from your life because you're too busy worrying and judging. Once you let go of that self-judgment, and embrace yourself...such magical things can happen. Love Your Body is like a comforting best friend, full of great advice and plenty of hugs when things get tough. I HIGHLY recommend reading it and sharing it with your girlfriends, and family."

✱ from Erin Kelly of blueyurtfarms.com

"This self-defeating society driven attitude of body hate is an absolute travesty, Which is why I think Love Your Body is such an important piece of work. Read it. If not for yourself, read it for the future generation of adult women in your life, your daughters, nieces and granddaughters. Read it to save them from a lifetime of feeling like they don't measure up. Read it so they can grow up knowing they are beautiful."

✱ from Jennah Scofield of housebarnfarm.com

DISCLAIMER

The information in this guide is for informational purposes only. Therefore, if you wish to apply ideas contained in this book, you are taking full responsibility for your actions.

I am not a medical doctor, and the information in this book is not intended as a substitute for the medical advice of a licensed physician. The reader should regularly consult a physician in matters relating to his/her health, particularly with respect to any symptoms that may require diagnosis or medical attention.

This book is not intended to be used, nor should it be used, to diagnose or treat any medical condition. Please consult your physician for diagnosis or treatment of any medical problem. The author is not responsible for any specific health or allergy needs that may require medical supervision and is not liable for any damages or negative consequences resulting from any action by a person reading or following the information in this book.

The references provided are for informational purposes only and do not constitute endorsement of any sources.

ABOUT THIS BOOK

I'm Elizabeth Walling, and you may know me from my blog *The Nourished Life* where I've been writing about health and wellness since 2009.

I believe there are a lot of components to living a nourished life. The way we live, eat, sleep and exercise can have a huge impact on our health. But so can the way we *think*—and that's where loving your body becomes a key factor.

For as long as I can remember, I did the whole yo-yo dieting thing, trying to "fix" my body. And let me tell you, I struggled with body hate every step of the way. No matter how much weight I lost, I never felt like I had "arrived" at the finish line. Whatever weight I was at, it was never good enough. In fact, the more rigid I became in my weight loss efforts, the more critical I became of my body. I noticed flaws I'd never paid attention to before, and thinking about these flaws all the time made me a pretty miserable person!

I finally decided I did not want to spend my life obsessed with my appearance. Some women struggle with body hate for 20 or 30 years or more, and I realized that's not the life I want to live. By this time, I'd committed to nourishing my body and taking care of it; and I knew that I couldn't truly do that if I didn't let go of body hate.

I wrote this book because I think it's important to enjoy life and live it to the fullest—but that's *really* hard to do when you hate your body! You see, body hate sort of seeps into every crevice of our lives and haunts us

even during what should be our happiest moments. It steals our joy out from under us because we're too busy focusing on our imperfections to appreciate the good things in life.

As I've learned to let go of negative body thoughts, life has taken on a whole new meaning. I never really understood how much body hate was holding me back until I learned to love my body (even if it *still* isn't perfect!).

In this book, I hope to pass on the ideas that have helped me the most during the last few years. I'll share the body-image myths that keep you trapped in body hate, the thinking patterns you can change to start feeling better about your body, and specific steps you can take to nourish yourself and take care of your body.

At the end of each chapter, there's an action step you can take to help make what you've learned stick. They're all short and to the point, and shouldn't take more than a few minutes. But if you do them, you might be surprised at the impact they have. (Having a notebook for these short exercises can be helpful so

you can have something to refer back to as you work through this book.)

Keep in mind that all the ideas you find here are meant to be flexible and adaptable to your life. Learning to love your body is a journey that takes some time and patience—and it doesn't happen overnight. Small, consistent changes make a *big* difference over time. As the famous quote goes, "A journey of a thousand miles begins with a single step."

✳ *Elizabeth*

TABLE OF CONTENTS

1
WHY LOVE YOUR BODY?

"Why love the unlovable?" That seems to be the underlying thought hiding deep down in the heart of the modern woman. So instead of working to love, respect, and appreciate their bodies, women declare war on their physical selves.

We will pinch, squeeze, starve, style, and surgically sculpt our bodies. Some of us even give up, throw our hands in the air, and resort to merely hiding our bodies under yoga pants, sweat shirts, and dresses four sizes too big.

But to *love* your body? Unthinkable!

YOU ARE WHAT YOU THINK ABOUT YOUR BODY

Body hate tends to penetrate our lives in ways we could never have predicted. We think we're just concerned with a few flaws; but when negative body thoughts invade our thinking and eventually our decisions, body hate can take its toll.

Why? Because you *are* what you focus on and what holds your attention. The way you think about something will dictate the decisions you make about it. Eventually, this begins to change the course of your life and your relationships with the people in your life.

WHAT IS BODY HATE COSTING YOU?

Most women keep a daily tab running of all the reasons their imperfections are holding them back.

- "If I didn't have so much cellulite, then I could wear shorts."

- "If I could lose those last twenty pounds, then I would have the confidence to start dating again."

- "If I didn't have any pimples, then I wouldn't need to hide my face at work."

But the truth is, hating your body for its imperfection is holding you back a heck of a lot more than the imperfections themselves.

Body hate has a cost. It can cost you money, that's true; but it can also cost you time. And more importantly, body hate can steal your peace of mind and enjoyment of life. The cost of body hate escalates when you allow your negative body image to dictate your decisions. Suddenly your body hate is in charge of your life, telling you what you're allowed to do and where you're allowed to go. It wraps you up in chains and prevents you from being able to live the life you want to live.

So what is hating your body really costing you? Go through the checklist below and see if you recognize any of these consequences of body hate:

- Anger toward yourself and your body.

- Shame about the way you look.

- Jealously toward people you think are better looking.

- Fear of rejection.

- Disgust about the way you look.

- Avoidance of intimate relationships because you're afraid to let someone too close to your imperfections.

- Stress on your close relationships.

- Avoidance of activities related to your body (like going to the beach or pool).

- Avoidance of social activities (like parties or eating out with friends).

- Isolation and loneliness as because of avoiding social situations and intimate relationships.

- Avoidance of getting your picture taken or being in photographs.

- Excessive time spent exercising, even to the point of increased risk of injury.

- Excessive time spent getting dressed, putting on makeup, fixing your hair.

- Excessive money spent on beauty products, slimming or cellulite creams, hair products, etc., which promise to fix your imperfections.

Can you think of other ways your body-hate detracts from your life?)

The problem is, we typically blame these feelings and behaviors on the imperfection itself. But the shape of your nose, the dimples in your thighs, or the size of your pants aren't actually *causing* any of these problems.

So if your imperfections aren't the problem, then what *is* the problem? **The way you *think* about your imperfections is the real problem.** (I'll go into more detail about this in later chapters.)

THE BENEFITS OF LOVING YOUR BODY

Just as body hate has consequences, loving your body has its benefits. **In fact, if you can really come to a place where you love, accept, and respect your body, it can**

completely change your outlook on life. Read through these questions and really think about the answers.

If you loved your body...

...would you feel more confident and at ease with yourself?

...would you feel more free and able to go after what you really want?

...would you have more time and money for things that bring enjoyment to your life?

...would it improve your relationships with your family and friends?

...would you have more energy to pursue relationships and activities that would add meaning to your life?

BODY HATE: A BIG FAT DISTRACTION

Let's face it: life can sometimes feel like one huge laundry list of problems. And many of them are painful to face, require a lot of time and effort to change, and occasionally are just plain unsolvable. But you are conveniently provided with one endless distraction from these problems, somewhere you can

always shift the blame, something you can always try to fix: your body.

Body hate can consume us, sometimes to the point where **every problem becomes a body problem.** Often when you're feeling uncomfortable, anxious, or angry, these feelings may not *initially* be about your body; but you end up directing them *toward* your body. Instead of digging deep and facing what's really bothering you, it's easier to just blame your body. This gives you something else to fix, something else to focus on—but it also prevents you from dealing with the real issues. So you remain trapped in the cycle of body hate, while problems that need your attention are neglected, and therefore go unresolved.

GET TO THE ROOT OF THE PROBLEM

Try this word game: take your negative body thoughts and turn them into thoughts about yourself or your life. Does something ring true?

My body is unacceptable. —> **I** *am unacceptable.*

No could love this body. —> *No one could love* **me**.

*My body is so weak and useless. —> **I** am so weak and useless.*

*They will reject my body. —> They will reject **me**.*

*I am so disappointed with my body. —> I am so disappointed with **my life**.*

Negative body thoughts sometimes appear to come out of nowhere; but next time you find yourself struggling with body hate, stop and think about what happened around the time you started feeling suddenly hateful toward your body. Did you have an argument with your mom? Are you feeling pressured at work? Did your spouse make a comment that really bothered you?

Ask yourself, "Is something else in my life making me uncomfortable (or anxious or guilty)?" Chances are, **you started feeling that way about your body because something else triggered a negative emotion.**

When we pause to question the source of our negative body thoughts, we can gain some key insights into what's really bothering us. And when we find the source of our troubles, we can take steps to address the real issues.

DON'T PASS IT ON

Body hate spreads like a contagious disease, but we're often fooled into thinking that when we hate our bodies, we're only hurting ourselves (which is bad enough). The truth is that body hate has an impact on those around us as well.

Do you have kids? They say that our children are like our little mirrors—it's only natural that they imitate the ones they look up to. They learn by example and pick up on our little idiosyncrasies—like the way we laugh or how we scrunch our eyebrows when we're trying to solve a problem. But this means our kids can also learn about body image through our behavior toward our own bodies. Do they see you go on diet after diet? Do they watch you criticize your body every time you look in the mirror? Do they hear you make ugly body comments? You know the ones—like "ugh, my thunder thighs won't fit in these shorts" or "I hate my arms; they're so hairy!"

So when you're tempted to wallow in body hate, think for a minute about how you want your kids to feel

about their bodies (or if you don't have kids, how you'd like your best friend to feel). I bet you'd love them to feel beautiful, confident, capable, strong, and all of those good things. If you do, that's another great reason for *you* to learn to feel that way, too.

TAKE ACTION!

Imagine you've lived to the ripe old age of ninety, and you decide to write your memoirs. What do you want them to say? What would you want people to remember about you? That you had perfectly sculpted abs? That your makeup was always done so well?

Or would you rather be remembered for your generous spirit, for your graciousness, for your passion for life? That you enjoyed life, lived it to the fullest, and made people laugh?

And what did you *do* during your long life? Did you travel? Meet interesting people? Eat exotic foods? Write a novel? Start a farm?

Or did you spend hours every day worried about how your jeans were fitting and anxious about the

lines forming around your eyes? Did you spend a small fortune on spa treatments, skin creams, and diet pills trying to "fix" your body?

When you look back on your life, what do you think will mean the most to you? **The way you look might be lower on the priority list than you realize.**

Write it down. Write what you would really like to say about your life and yourself if you lived to the age of ninety. It might just be the catalyst you need to change how you think about your body.

2
BUSTING BODY-IMAGE MYTHS

Our culture is infused with myths about what we should expect from our bodies and how we should feel about them. Some of these myths stem from the unrealistic standards portrayed by the modern media, others are born out of the pursuit of perfectionism, and still more rise from the holes riddled in our self-esteem when we were growing up.

But however the seeds of these myths were planted, it's high time we recognize and dispel the false ideas we have about body image so we can make way for a more positive mindset.

BODY-IMAGE MYTHS

✗ Myth

My body isn't me.

✔ Truth

Your body may not be the *whole* you, but it is definitely a part of you. Rejecting (or ignoring) your body is rejecting part of yourself. And I probably don't have to tell you that rejection (even from yourself) is painful and can lead to negative emotions like shame, guilt, and discouragement.

So no more ignoring and rejecting your body! Instead, we're going to work on developing more positive attitudes that help you learn how to embrace your body's unique qualities, appreciate its capabilities, and accept its imperfections.

✗ Myth

Hating my body will help motivate me to make the problem go away.

✔ **Truth**

Hating your body will only make your problems seem even worse. Body hate doesn't solve any problems or make imperfections go away. Instead, it fuels negative emotions that keep us thinking about the problem, noticing it, and worrying about it. Body hate isn't motivating—it's agonizing. It only serves to make your imperfections seem more important than the rest of your life and fools you into thinking that you should put more time, energy, and effort into "fixing" your body instead of living your life.

✗ **Myth**

I'll love my body later (when it's thin, or cellulite-free, or tan, or has more curves, or has less hair, etc.).

✔ **Truth**

If you don't learn to love and accept your body as it is right now in this moment, you probably won't love it even if your imperfections suddenly disappeared. I know, you're probably thinking, "Yeah, right! My flaws

are my problem. If they were gone, my body hate would be gone, too."

But think about it: body hate is a learned thinking pattern. It's a mindset. **Even if your imperfections were gone, if you still had the *mindset* of body hate, then you would still hate your body.**

For instance, let's say you want to lose weight to feel better about yourself. Even if you are able to change your body by losing weight, you have to learn to respect and accept your body along the way. Should you really be waiting until the scale says a certain number before you feel good about yourself? **Positive body image is a skill you need to practice**; and if you don't do it now, then you won't know how to do it even if you do lose weight.

Maybe you've been through this or seen someone you know go through it: you lose the 20 pounds you've always hoped to lose, only to suddenly be even more consumed with the size and shape of your body. You start to wonder if that tiny belly pooch would finally be gone if you could lose 10 more pounds. You pinch

your thighs, and think about that commercial you saw for an expensive cellulite treatment. Instead of being happy with the change you worked hard to achieve, you're now even more consumed with your appearance and your imperfections.

This can happen in even more extreme cases where someone resorts to cosmetic surgery to change their body. But soon after their first surgery, they start planning more surgeries to "tweak" the results or resolve other issues they were never concerned about before.

Body hate is a mindset; and it's not caused by the fact that your body isn't perfect, but by your *thoughts* about your imperfections.

✗ Myth

My body isn't normal. No one else has to deal with these problems. I just need to fix these issues so I can be normal too!

✔ Truth

Your body is totally normal! Whatever imperfection

you feel plagues you, it's plagued thousands—if not millions—of women before you. *Every* person has imperfections, which means that imperfections are not only normal, but should be expected!

"Normal" comes in all shapes and sizes, with countless variations. Some women have more cellulite; others have less. Some have wide hips; others have wide shoulders. Some have a bump at the end of their nose; some don't. Some have fine hair, and some have thick hair. Some tend to gain weight easily; others have a hard time gaining weight even if they really want to.

So whatever the case is for you, **don't let a narrow definition of "normal" make you feel like your body isn't worth loving.**

✗ Myth

Life would be easier if I had the right body! My work, my romantic relationships, and my own confidence would all be better if my body didn't have these issues.

✔ **Truth**

The importance of appearance is often blown way out of proportion. I won't sugar coat it: there is a grain of truth in the idea that how you look affects how other people respond to you in situations like work and romantic relationships. But when it comes to succeeding in life and being happy with yourself, how you look doesn't even come close to being as important as how you feel about yourself.

It doesn't matter how you look—whether you fit the modern standard for beauty or not—**you are holding yourself back** if you are ashamed of your body, if you hide from social situations because you aren't comfortable in your own skin, or if you're constantly seeking reassurance from loved ones about the way you look.

Confidence, perseverance, passion, grace, and other positive qualities are built from the inside out. There are plenty of people who you might consider to have the ideal body, but who also have zero self-

confidence and fail to live the life they want because of their negative body image.

✗ Myth

I need acceptance from others to feel good about my body.

✔ Truth

You need acceptance from *yourself* to feel good about your body. What others think about your body doesn't affect your confidence half as much as what *you* think about your body.

People suffer from negative body thoughts even when everyone around them thinks they're beautiful. And if you learn to embrace your body, then suddenly what others think doesn't matter as much. **Let your confidence show from the inside out, and others will get the message.**

✗ Myth

I feel ugly, so I must be ugly.

✔ Truth

Feeling something doesn't make it true. Feelings are fickle things and fluctuate at the slightest influence. A negative comment from a family member or trying on one pair of ill-fitting pants might be enough to take you from feeling fine about your body to thinking you look absolutely terrible. So what changed? Not your body—it's the same body you had five minutes ago when you felt fine. **What changed were the thoughts you're thinking about your body.**

Your general mood can also impact how you feel about your body. On a good day, your imperfections probably don't seem like a big deal. But if you're under stress at work or had a fight with your mom on the phone, suddenly everything in your life is colored with negative emotions. And if you tend to focus energy on negative body thoughts, then these thoughts will naturally come to the surface when you're in a bad mood.

The next time you feel an episode of body hate coming on, ask yourself if something else is influencing your emotions. Don't take those negative

body thoughts too seriously, and remind yourself that this mood will pass.

✗ Myth

If I stop thinking so much about the problem, it will just get even worse.

✔ Truth

Letting go of body hate doesn't mean letting yourself go, but it does mean letting go of thoughts and behaviors that detract from your life. Most people feel that letting go of body obsession is like letting a monster loose. It feels like if you stop weighing yourself several times a day, your weight will skyrocket. Or you might feel like if you didn't touch up your makeup every ten minutes, people won't be able to stop looking at your acne scars.

But chances are, these behaviors are actually *feeding* your body hate. They keep you focused on the imperfection and give you the illusion of control, when really your negative body thoughts are controlling

you. These behaviors also blow every imperfection out of proportion. Gaining half a pound or finding a new pimple will feel like the end of the world, when in reality these are *normal* occurrences that are bound to happen now and then to everybody!

TAKE ACTION!

So a magic genie grants you a wish. *Bam!* You now have the body you always wanted. Now, close your eyes and take a moment to really imagine how you would feel.

- Would you feel more confident?

- Would you feel more outgoing?

- Would you feel more respected?

- Would you feel more graceful?

- Would you smile more?

- Would you try something new?

- Would you speak your mind more often?

When you say you want a better body, you usually mean that changing your body would solve another

problem in your life. What you really want is not just to change your body, but to change the way you feel or behave.

Changing your body doesn't necessarily solve other problems in your life. After all, there are plenty of people you might consider beautiful who don't feel confident, who don't speak their mind, or who don't feel respected.

From now on, think about what you *really* want and then brainstorm about what might help you reach those goals even without changing your body.

3
STUCK IN THE WAITING ROOM

Imagine you're in a waiting room full of people. There's a heavy wooden door in the corner of the room with the word "PERFECT" in brass letters across the front. Theoretically, someone should open the door every few moments and call out a name to let someone know their body is finally good enough to move forward in life. The trouble is, the door never opens. Everyone is stuck in the waiting room.

At first, you and the others in the room don't think much about it. After all, this is just the way things are. Life can only be enjoyed by the perfectly beautiful, and everyone just accepts this fact. But then the waiting room starts to get stuffy. People begin to fidget in their chairs. You're tired of waiting to find out what's behind that door.

There's murmuring between some of the others now. Who gets to determine who's good enough to walk through that door? What does "perfect" mean anyway? Why can't everyone pursue their dreams? What's stopping you?

Finally, one woman wrenches a metal nail file from her purse. She runs up to the door and shoves the file under each letter of the word "PERFECT" until they fall to the floor one by one. Someone else shouts that she should jimmy the lock, but when she grabs the knob, it opens effortlessly. It was never locked at all.

Everyone in the waiting room crowds around the door in awe of what lays beyond. It's nothing like they imagined. There are people everywhere—startlingly *imperfect* people—enjoying their lives.

An elderly gentleman in green running shorts and a

striped athletic head band spots you and waves. He smiled and says, "Come on out! What are you waiting for?"

Good question. What *are* you waiting for?

THE PERFECTIONISM TRAP

Perfectionism is often to blame when we get stuck waiting to pursue our dreams until we have the "right" body. But perfectionism locks us in a trap where everything might happen *someday* when conditions are *just* right, but that perfect "someday" never seems to arrive.

The perfectionist attitude makes sweeping judgments and jumps to extremes. Perfectionism says, "I'm not everything I want to be, so therefore I am nothing." It says if you're not perfect, you're worthless. Life just isn't worth living to the fullest if you can't do it with the perfect skin, the perfect hair, the perfect thighs...

Really? Who says? It's time to put a brake on the perfectionist mindset and question whether or not

it's legitimate. To do that, you need to ask yourself questions like these:

- Is there really a rule that only people with "perfect" legs can wear shorts? Who made that rule? And who decides what perfect legs are, anyway?

- Is it really insane to leave the house without tons of makeup? Who says you have to cake on the concealer to cover your wrinkles or acne scars? Do you really only deserve to be seen when you're hiding your skin?

- Why can't you go on vacation until you lose 20 pounds? Is the sun setting over the sandy shores of Aruba somehow *less* beautiful if you're above a certain number on the scale? Are only people of a certain size supposed to take a break from life and enjoy some time for themselves?

You may be asking, "Shouldn't I put my best face forward?" or "Is it wrong to try to improve my body in any way?" I'll address this in more detail in Chapter

8, but for now I'll just say this: **there is a tremendous difference between taking steps to improve certain aspects of ourselves, and putting our life completely on hold until we reach those goals.**

Don't hide behind the fear of being imperfect. We're *all* imperfect! Every other person who has worn a bikini, asked someone out on a date, or learned to swing dance had physical imperfections—some even had the very same imperfections as you do!

LIVING IN THE NOW

The problem with negative body thoughts is they distract you from living in the moment and actually experiencing your life. You're always thinking about what your body *used* to look like, what you *want* it to look like, what you *don't* want it to look like. So instead of relishing the feel of a spring breeze, you're caught up thinking about how many pounds you need to lose before bathing suit season.

Body hate not only postpones life until you "fix"

your body, it also steals enjoyment from your everyday life by keeping you fixated on everything you don't like about your body.

Fortunately, this process can work in reverse. If you practice living in the moment, it can keep those negative body thoughts at bay. Try this:

- Stop what you're doing and close your eyes if you can.

- Breathe in slowly and take a minute to really feel yourself breathing.

- Open your eyes and take in the moment. Use all of your senses to experience it.

- What noises do you hear? What colors do you see? What draws your eye and grabs your attention? If you're holding something (a pencil, a coffee mug, a computer mouse), how does it feel in your hand?

- Is someone talking to you? Are you really listening? Could you pay more attention and play a more active role in the conversation?

Anytime you feel disconnected from the moment or if you're overcome with thoughts of body hate, do

this exercise to pull yourself back into the moment and experience what is really going on around you.

Doing this can help you avoid getting caught up in negative body thoughts, and can also help you focus on what really needs your attention in life.

TAKE ACTION!

Sit down and make a list of everything you want to do but have been putting it off because you're not happy with your body. Here are some ideas that may strike a chord:

- Go to the beach.

- Wear shorts.

- Get a hairstyle that emphasizes your face instead of hiding it.

- Do yoga.

- Try speed dating.

- Buy a sexy, red dress.

- Go after that promotion.

- Learn to surf.

- Wear lingerie that actually fits and flatters your figure.

- Shop for a bathing suit.

- Go dancing.

- Speak in front of a group of people.

- Go hiking in the mountains.

Can you think of any others?

Now, make a goal to do at least one thing on your list this month. Just one. See how it feels. Then do it again next month. **Start making plans that don't hinge on you changing your body first.**

Remember, thousands of people do these things every day, and none of them have perfect bodies. You don't have to have a certain body type to do things that make your life interesting and fulfilling. Start today!

4
FOOLED BY FAKE

- Letting go of body hate is impossible if you're convinced that if you just tried hard enough, you could make your imperfections disappear.

- Most of us believe this myth on some level or another when we accept the idea that the perfect body exists in the real world.

- In order to banish negative body thoughts into the abyss where they belong, we have to break free from the false idea that "perfection" actually exists.

THERE IS NO PERFECT

Our culture of glossy magazine covers, diet pills, and skin creams wants you to believe that the perfect body is not only possible, but even reasonably attainable.

This is—for lack of a better term—a big, fat lie. But we buy into the myth because it's *everywhere*. Seeing is believing, and we see evidence that the perfect body can exist almost everywhere we look. Ads on the internet, pictures in magazines, movies on the big screen, romance novel covers, protein supplement labels... the "ideal" body is plastered in so many places, it seems like proof that it must exist somewhere. And if other people have this body (and surely they do, right?), then we assume that *we* should be able to have that body, too.

PHOTOSHOP LIES AND OTHER ILLUSIONS

The perfect body isn't *real*. It's a hypothetical idea. It's dreamed up and then brought to life by a myriad of extreme measures that make perfection appear harmonious with reality. But don't be fooled.

Perfection and reality are just about as far apart as this galaxy and the next.

All media images and messages are constructions. They are not reflections of reality. Advertisements and other media messages have been carefully crafted with the intent to send a very specific message.

✻ PBS.org.

Just think of all the elaborate steps it takes to get the flawless photo on the magazine cover:

- The model or actress on the cover has likely been on a strict diet and exercise regimen leading up to the photo shoot (yes, even professional models often have to diet to get "that" look—it's really that unsustainable).

- Next comes a circus of artists formally trained to erase imperfections with makeup, hair styling and everything in between.

- When it comes time to shoot the photo, even all this preparation won't cut it. Now lighting has

to be *just* right and even special camera lenses can be used to alter how the image turns out.

- Good enough? Not by a long shot. Now the real specialists come it to bring the image up to industry standards with photo editing software. Tiny wrinkles around the eyes? Erased. Hair can be lengthened, a few inches can be skimmed off the waist, another few off the outer thighs... sometimes the entire image is distorted or stretched to change a person's body size or height. Skin tone can be darkened or lightened. (Anyone want a California tan?) Eyes can be widened or the color altered. Basically, there is no end to the alterations that can be done to a photo before it finally reaches the pages of a magazine.

- By the time you see the image on the cover in the checkout aisle of the grocery store, you're looking at a picture of someone who doesn't even exist in the real world, in spite of the fact

that every page of the magazine will tell us we can look like that person if we try.

WHAT USED-CAR SHOPPING SAYS ABOUT BEAUTY

Let's say you're shopping for a used car. At the far end of the car lot, you spot it: the orange sports car you've always wanted. You're almost giddy when you realize how incredible it looks up close. The paint gleams and the windows sparkle. You're starting to feel pretty lucky.

You take a quick pass around the car and it looks superb. The mileage isn't too bad (though the price is slightly above budget), so you decide to take it for a test drive. But as you spend a little time with the car, you start to notice an imperfection here or there. The plastic in the dash looks a little faded on the edges, and there's a small gash in the armrest.

By the time you get back to the car lot and take another look around the exterior, you realize the car's not in that great of shape, after all. There are scuff marks on the left fender (someone tried to squeeze into a tight

parking space?) and a couple paint chips on the front hood (loose gravel from the highway, maybe). The tread on the tires is looking a little worn down, too. Overall, it's not in terrible shape, but it's definitely not the image of perfection you considered it a few minutes ago.

The point is that things may *look* perfect at first glance or if you're not looking too closely, but they usually aren't. **Perfection is an illusion that seems nice on the surface, but it just isn't reality.** And anyone who goes through life expecting perfection from their body (or anything else) is bound to be disappointed a whole lot.

QUESTION YOUR STANDARDS

Instead of following along with a media-driven standard for beauty, why not set your own standards? If you balk at the idea of breaking away from a limited definition of beauty, ask yourself these questions:

- **Do your current standards for beauty work in your life?** Or do they always have you chasing

perfection, never being fully happy with where you are? Do your standards allow you to make room in your life for other important ventures that need your time and energy?

- **Are your standards positive?** Or do they revolve around what you *aren't* or what you *shouldn't* be? Do they have you ticking off a list of flaws instead of thinking about your assets?

- **Are your standards of beauty realistic?** Or are you trying to live up to the kind of beauty defined by constant restriction, professional makeup artists, and heavy photo editing?

- **Do they matter *now*?** Are you holding on to a beauty ideal you adopted as a child or young adult? Do you think those standards apply to your life, your goals, and your needs right now?

TAKE ACTION!

What does "beautiful" mean? Instead of seeking the answer from the media, beauty should be something we

define within ourselves. When we set our own standards for beauty, suddenly the word *beautiful* becomes fluid and liberating instead of oppressive and confining.

Sometimes it's hard to define beauty when we're so wrapped up in our flaws and sore spots. Instead, start by looking outside yourself.

> [N]ame the people you know that you find beautiful. What is it that makes them so beautiful to you? Do you use the same standard when judging yourself?

✳ Rosie Molinary, *Beautiful You.*

Now write down a list. What *is* beauty to you? Is it just a collection of nicely assembled body parts? Or is it something more? Does beauty start from the inside out? For instance, should any of the qualities below be considered beautiful?

- compassion

- laughter

- grace

- thoughtfulness

- kindness

- courage
- unconditional love
- adventurous spirit
- spontaneity
- sincerity
- ambition
- persistence
- curiosity
- loyalty
- strength
- sensuality
- generosity

5
STOP BODY-BASHING

Sometimes we get fooled into thinking something is okay just because it's normal. But normal isn't good enough. We have to examine thoughts and behaviors that may be considered "normal" and ask ourselves: does this serve a positive function in my life?

When it comes to body-bashing, the answer is a resounding *"NO!"*

Body-bashing couldn't be more normal. It's not only accepted in our culture, but it's even encouraged. Sometimes, it's the only way we know how to relate to our physical bodies, or the primary way we bond with friends and family. **But that doesn't change the fact that body-bashing is absolutely and irrevocably *wrong*.**

STOP UGLY BODY THOUGHTS

Body-bashing starts in our heads. These ugly body thoughts are so pervasive and habitual we often don't realize how mean and cruel we are to our bodies. Growing up, most of us learned the rule that name-calling is a no-no. But most of us think that calling *ourselves* names doesn't really count. We say things to ourselves that we would never dream of saying to a friend or even a stranger. And somehow we think it's okay to treat ourselves this way, to deem ourselves unworthy of common courtesy.

Basic human decency doesn't just apply to others—it applies to you, too. And when your thoughts are filled with a constant stream of ugly body talk, it's going to be awfully hard to develop a positive attitude toward yourself and your life.

You know the thoughts I'm talking about:

- "I hate these cottage-cheese thighs!"

- "Ugh, I can't stand looking at myself today. Can you see that muffin top?! That is so gross!"

- "My nose is so ugly. I look like a freak!"

- "I'm such a fat cow. I don't even deserve to eat."

Really, how can you hope to be happy in life if these thoughts running through your mind every time you look in the mirror? It's an uphill battle, that's for sure (some might say darn near impossible!).

LEARN TO DETECT UGLY BODY THOUGHTS

To change this dynamic, you have to work from the inside out. The first step is simply recognizing when you experience ugly body thoughts. Tune into what you say to yourself about your body, and then think about what events are triggering negative body thoughts. (We'll talk more about that in the next chapter).

At first you might not catch the ugly body thoughts until you've been thinking that way for several minutes

or more; but eventually, you'll start picking up on it right away.

When you encounter those ugly body thoughts, you have to fight back. Body hate is often fueled by emotional assumptions and distorted thinking. The trick is to unravel this web of thinking by questioning whether these thoughts are legitimate.

Ask yourself these questions:

- Does this thought represent reality, or could my perception be skewed?

- Am I thinking in extremes or blowing something out of proportion?

- Is there another way to look at this issue?

- Could I do something to improve the way I feel right now?

Here are a couple examples of how to counter those ugly body thoughts:

Ugly Body Thought...

"Ugh, I can't stand looking at myself today. Can you see that muffin top?! I am so gross!"

Look at it This Way Instead...

"Okay, so maybe I'm not thrilled with the way my stomach looks right now. I guess it doesn't help that I'm wearing low-cut pants that don't sit right on my body. Besides, even if my stomach doesn't look the way I want it to, that doesn't make me 'gross'—it just means I'm a person with imperfections just like everyone else. Who cares if my stomach isn't perfect? I do have nice legs, and maybe I'll wear that dress that shows them off instead!"

Ugly Body Thought...

"I'm such a fat cow. I don't even deserve to eat."

Look at it This Way Instead...

"It's true, my weight isn't where I want it to be. But that is not an excuse to call myself ugly names. I can't let my self-worth depend entirely on the shape of my

body. It's also not an excuse to starve myself. Maybe sometimes I eat for reasons other than physical hunger, and that's something I can work on. In the meantime, I'm a living human being so, yes, I do deserve to eat.

Besides, I already know that denying myself food will eventually lead to binging; and then the whole negative cycle starts all over again, so that is not a healthy or balanced approach for me."

STOP UGLY BODY TALK

Body hate is perceived as normal, but it doesn't have to be. Part of what keeps body hate alive and kicking is the fact that it's an acceptable topic of conversation. Not only that, but sometimes we actually relish in a good body-bashing session with friends!

Sometimes we don't even realize how much body hate has become the center of our conversations. The fact is, we all want to relate to each other; and unfortunately, body hate is a subject most of us have personal experience with.

Think about it: how often do you and your friends

talk about how much you hate your stomach or your butt or your arms? Are you always discussing the latest diet or exercise craze? Do you talk about how many pounds you've gained or lost, how many gray hairs you found this week?

Observe your conversations with friends and family, and see how much you *really* talk about your appearance in a negative way. You might be surprised and even a little saddened when you realize how central body hate has been to your discussions.

"Well, it's all true. Why not talk about it?" you might say.

Sure, it might be true that you don't like certain things about your body. But constantly giving your flaws center stage isn't painting truthful picture either.

Your imperfections certainly aren't the sum of who you are, but talking too much about your flaws gives them more power than they deserve.

Instead, why not talk about why you feel it's so important to stop body-bashing? After all, if body hate is such a central issue, your friends can probably relate

to the negative feelings that often result from ugly body talk. An honest discussion about the alternatives to body hate can take the conversation in a much more meaningful and positive direction.

THE WORLD WIDE WEB OF BODY HATE

Aside from friends and family, body-bashing also boils over onto the internet. Put people behind the safety of a computer screen; and all of the sudden, they feel free to let loose every cruel and insensitive remark imaginable—especially in the case of appearance.

Body hate is everywhere on the web... all over forums, blogs, and social media sites. There are thousands of groups online that foster body obsession. There are forums devoted to acne cures, plastic surgery, fad diets, extreme exercise and just about any other body-related topic. And all of them encourage commiserating over our flaws and going down endless rabbit holes trying to "fix" our bodies.

The truth is, these groups rarely provide real

solutions. They only serve to trigger our insecurities and make our problems seem even bigger than they really are. What's more, they show us that body hate is normal and acceptable—hating your body is just part of fitting in.

This isn't a problem for everyone, but it's important to stop and think about how your online relationships are affecting your life.

- Do you feel better or worse after visiting sites or groups that frequently discuss body issues, appearance, dieting, or exercise?

- Do you come away feeling more at peace or more anxious about the way you look?

Not all groups and web sites foster body hate. Some even encourage positive body image. Just be sure you know which ones you're involved with. **Take the time to honestly assess your online activity and cut out the influences that promote body hate.** It can make a huge difference in banishing ugly body thoughts.

TAKE ACTION!

Get a sheet of paper and a pen. We're going to dig deep and bring all that ugly body talk out into the light of day.

Write down every single derogatory comment you say to yourself about your body. If you have a difficult time thinking of any, imagine what you think when you look in the mirror first thing in the morning, or when you go shopping for jeans.

Read your list of negative body thoughts out loud. Seriously, don't skip out on that part. You need to *hear* the true weight of these words that you haphazardly tell yourself on a daily basis. How awful do they really sound?

After you've read through your thoughts and said them out loud, now it's time to put them where they belong. Crumple up that paper and throw it in the garbage can.

You are done with those thoughts. You've wasted enough time and energy thinking negative thoughts about your body. It's time to throw out this pattern of thinking.

Every time you catch yourself thinking one of those thoughts from the list (or something like it), picture yourself writing it down and throwing it away—or if you need to, actually write it down and banish that paper to the garbage. Tell those thoughts, "You're being evicted. You don't get to rent space in my head anymore!"

6
DON'T READ MINDS (OR TELL FORTUNES)

You know how a fish tank has a filter to keep the fish from being assaulted by icky stuff? If the filter isn't working, the water can get ugly fast. Our minds also have a sort of filter, but the trouble is that sometimes it doesn't work so well. In fact, some of us are filtering out the good stuff and letting bad stuff run loose!

Body hate often stems from not seeing the big picture. We see things through a negative filter that blocks out the positive aspects of a situation. When that happens, all the negative stuff feels ten times worse, because there's no positive point of view to balance it out. We only notice our flaws, our weak points, and our shortcomings. Any positive aspects of ourselves are discounted or explained away.

- "Who cares if I got promoted? Someone had to fill the position. It doesn't mean I'm special. A promotion doesn't change the fact that I look old and frumpy."

- "He said I looked pretty today, but he probably noticed I was in a bad mood and was just trying to be nice. He didn't really mean it."

A negative thought filter means that what we think about ourselves (and what we assume others think about us) isn't always realistic. In fact, it's usually charged with negative emotion and a history of body hate.

The good news is we can change our filters. With some practice, you can learn to assess your body and situations from a *balanced* perspective that looks at both sides of an issue, instead of just assuming the worst.

STOP MIND READING

A lot of body image angst comes from our feeble attempts at mind reading. Sure, part of you knows that you can't read people's minds, but the other part is still convinced that you know what other people think about you. Specifically, they hate the way you look. And you're sure of it.

> Whenever you mind read, you make assumptions that you know what other people are thinking. And because you are so sure what the other person thinks, you don't even bother to check it out.

> Of course, people sometimes do make negative judgments about one another. But this probably occurs less often than you think. In many cases, your theories about what others are thinking about your appearance are either wrong or blown out of proportion.

> ✳ Sabine Wilhelm, PhD,
> *Feeling Good About the Way You Look.*

When you catch yourself mind reading, don't just accept your assumptions as truth. Evaluate your thoughts and see if they line up with reality. Ask yourself questions like:

- What is the evidence that this is true?

- Is this a realistic assumption?

- Are there other possibilities?

Here's how this might play out in the real world:

Negative Assumption

"He said I looked pretty today, but he probably noticed I was in a bad mood and was just trying to be nice. He didn't really mean it."

Evaluation

Q. What is the evidence that this is true?

A. I can't think of any evidence, to be honest. I'm just guessing.

Q. Is this a realistic assumption?

A. Not really. I have no reason to think he would lie just to make me feel better. He's actually a pretty straightforward person.

Q. *Are there other possibilities?*

A. Yes, he could have genuinely meant it as a compliment. Even if he did say it to be nice, that doesn't mean he doesn't believe I look pretty today.

STOP FORTUNE TELLING

Right along with mind reading, most of us seem to think we can predict the future as well. (Aren't we talented?) But usually, our predictions are sweeping generalizations that are wildly exaggerated extensions of a temporary negative emotion.

For example, you went through a breakup a few months ago, but now you'd like to start dating again. You even went on a blind date last weekend and you actually had a decent time. The problem is, it's been a couple of days and the guy hasn't called. In a matter of seconds, you go from thinking, "He probably won't

bother to call me at all; I bet my nose completely turned him off" to thinking "I'm ugly, and I'm always going to be alone and miserable."

From the outside, these predictions look kind of ridiculous; but many of us go through this downward spiral of negative thinking on a daily basis. Just like with mind reading, you need to question your fortune-telling ability and evaluate your thoughts. Ask yourself:

- What would a true friend tell me?

- What's the worst that could happen if my fears come true?

- Is there another way to look at this?

- Where can I go from here?

Negative Assumption

"He probably won't bother to call me at all; I bet my nose completely turned him off."

"I'm ugly, and I'm always going to be alone and miserable."

Evaluation

Q. What would a true friend tell me?

A. My best friend would say, "Yeah, right! First of all, you look great; and your date even went out of his way to say so. He's probably gonna call any minute now—it hasn't even been 48 hours, silly! And alone and miserable? Not if I can help it! Let's plan that trip to the beach we've been talking about doing for months."

Q. What's the worst that could happen if my fears come true?

A. Well, even if he doesn't call, I guess it's not the end of the world. It doesn't guarantee I'll be alone. True, I might end up alone for a while, but that doesn't mean I have to be miserable.

Q. Is there another way to look at this?

A. It was my first date in a while; and it was good to get out, regardless of whether or not this turns into a relationship. He might call back; but if not, I can't say that I know it was because of my nose. It could be for

any number of reasons. Maybe he just felt things didn't click between us. Maybe he's too busy with work to get involved with someone right now. Who knows?

Q. Where can I go from here?

A. I'm going to shrug this one off for now, and I'm definitely not waiting by the phone for anyone to call. I'm going to get out of the house and enjoy the beautiful weather we've been having.

You give complete control to ugly body thoughts when you automatically accept them as reality. When you make the effort to question and evaluate your thoughts, you take the power away from body hate and realize you have more control over how you feel than you realized.

TAKE ACTION!

Every day this week, practice "talking back" to your ugly body thoughts. Pick a negative body thought and write it down in a notebook. Answer that thought with a voice of reason by asking yourself the questions discussed in this chapter:

- What is the evidence that this is true?

- Is this a realistic assumption?

- Are there other possibilities?

- What would a true friend tell me?

- What's the worst that could happen if my fears come true?

- Is there another way to look at this?

- Where can I go from here?

Write down the answers in your notebook. After a week of talking back to ugly body thoughts, you'll see that you don't have to just sit back and accept all that body hate as truth. And you'll also have a small arsenal of ways you can respond to negative body thoughts whenever they hit you.

7
HOW TO LOVE YOUR BODY

- Love is more than a feeling. It's an *action* word.

- While it's important to have positive *feelings* toward your body, it's even better to take it a step further and put those feelings into *action*.

- If you have a hard time "feeling the love" for your body, taking steps toward *acting* in a way that's loving and respectful toward your body can help you get there.

- When you start taking care of yourself (both physically and emotionally), it actually gets easier to start appreciating your body on a new level.

- Even if you don't feel very friendly toward your body just yet, it may help to read through this chapter and start "going through the motions" until it starts to feel more natural.

LOVE MEANS LISTENING

We all know that one of the keys to a healthy relationship is good listening skills. When it comes to having a healthy relationship with your body, listening is also a top priority.

- You need to be tuned into your body's feedback if you want to take care of it.

- By listening to your body, you can home in on areas that need tweaking or find out if something you're doing just isn't working for you.

By paying attention to your body's needs and how it responds, you also learn to cooperate with your body and stop viewing it as the enemy who's out to get you.

Most of us have been battling our bodies for as long as we can remember. It's time to call a truce and let your body bring some valuable information to the table. You might be surprised at what it has to say.

FORGET THE PLAN

Listening to your body is a lost art. It's easy to get out of touch with your body's true needs when you're constantly pushed to follow the latest "plan" that tells you how to eat, how to move, even how to breathe. Plans always focus on the latest fads and buzz-words and rarely take into consideration whether or not something actually *works* for your body and in your life. You're just supposed to follow the plan. And if it doesn't work? Then you must not be doing it right!

So first things first: **forget the plan**.

- Start viewing any diet, exercise or lifestyle recommendation as a guideline, a starting place that you can adjust as needed.

- **Avoid extremes whenever possible.**

- Most of all, *pay attention to how your body responds and make adjustments as needed.*

KEYS TO LOVING YOUR BODY

1. No starving yourself. Starving your body is *not* loving it. Period. Skipping meals and crash dieting isn't healthy for you, physically or mentally. If you want to love your body, give it the energy it needs not only to survive, but to **thrive**. This means eating enough to support your lifestyle—so if you're active, eat enough to support that activity!

How much you need to eat will vary based on your body size, body type, and activity level; but most women need *at least* 2,000 calories a day. More importantly, **listen to your body**. If you're constantly hungry, thinking about food, or binge eating, *you are probably not eating enough.*

Moderation is fine, but restriction is not healthy. Avoid restricting food groups unless you have a genuine medical reason to do so.

2. Choose higher quality food. This isn't a diet book in any way, shape or form, so I won't go into great detail about food choices. But in general, go for the quality stuff. Focus on eating food in a more natural state. Avoid too much processed food or foods with lots of additives.

Keep it simple, keep it fresh. If you can, choose more organic foods and buy from local farmers who raise quality food the old-fashioned way. Aim for food with plenty of nutrients to support your body and mind.

But don't get too rigid! Enjoy a night out at a restaurant now and then without worrying about the exact ingredients. Eat the birthday cake at your friend's party. Eat well *most* of the time, but don't let it run your life.

3. Move your body in a way that brings you joy. Exercise should never be torture or used as punishment to make up for eating the "wrong" food or "too much" food.

Exercise is about feeling strong, healthy, vibrant, and moving your body in a way you enjoy. Being active is healthy, but there is such a thing as overdoing it,

especially if you're exhausted or not eating well. If that's the case, walking can sometimes be the most healing exercise until you're giving your body enough sleep and quality food to support more vigorous activity.

If you are eating and sleeping enough to support exercise, choose whatever activity makes you feel really positive about yourself and your body. This may be weight lifting or yoga or swimming or dancing—the choices are endless. Just do what you love. There are no rules.

4. Get plenty of sleep. Your body needs rest to recover and rebuild. Most people feel best on at least 7–9 hours of sleep every night. If you're regularly getting less than this, your body will suffer for it and will generally be a lot harder to work with, too!

If you want to feel rested, energized and youthful, a good night's sleep is a must. Prioritize sleep and take naps if needed to make sure you get your rest.

5. Make downtime a priority. Next to sleep, you should also try to incorporate a little downtime into

every day. Give your mind and body a chance to relax and not be under the constant strain of to-do lists and scheduled activities.

Take a break and make a little time every day to do something that rejuvenates you. Read a favorite book, sit out under the stars, walk in the woods, or watch a television show that makes you belly laugh. You'll feel better, trust me.

6. Accept compliments. Is this hard for you, too? I always find myself dodging or deflecting compliments. You know what I mean: they say, "I love your shirt"; and I reply, "Oh, I just threw something on this morning." Or they say, "Wow, your hair looks fantastic!" And I answer, "Oh, but I wish I had your hair!"

Compliments are a beautiful gift, and we should own them. If someone says you look wonderful, thank them and let them know that you really needed to hear that. If they compliment your shoes, you can tell them where you got them or how it's your favorite pair. Instead of letting compliments embarrass you, let them *empower* you!

7. Forgive yourself. Guilt and shame are negative emotions that steal our energy and motivation. They keep us focused on things we can't change. **The only way to move forward and make positive changes is to forgive ourselves.**

We can't change the past, but we can definitely do things differently in the future. Forgiving yourself is really *liberating* yourself and allowing you to put your energy into making better decisions in the future. And if you mess up, learn from your mistakes; but don't wallow in them. None of us are perfect, and we never will be. Move on and move forward.

8. Wear clothes you love. Loving your body means wearing clothes that you feel amazing! Women tend to be really hard on themselves when it comes to clothing. We feel like if we don't have the "ideal" body type then we'll never feel good in our clothes. But nothing could be further from the truth! Sure, everyone has a different size and shape to work with, but you really *can* find clothes that flatter your individual body type and express your unique personality.

Also, buy clothes for the body you have *now*. I've seen women refuse to buy *underwear* that fits because they want to lose weight first. That is *not* okay! You deserve underwear that fits and flatters.

Or worse, you buy clothes that are too tight, but *might* fit after you lose the proverbial ten pounds. **Wear what fits *your body as it is right now*.** If your size changes, then you can address that when the time comes. But you'll never feel good in your clothes if you're shopping for a body you don't have.

TAKE ACTION!

Make a list of three new ways you can start loving your body right away. Look back through this chapter and think about where you need to put more effort. Pick three different things you can start doing to love your body more and start working on them this week!

Here are a few examples:

1. Stop skipping meals. Eat a balanced meal or snack when I'm hungry instead.

2. Buy more fresh fruits to snack on. (Maybe go to the local farmer's market?)

3. Cut off the TV at 10:00 pm so I can get to sleep earlier.

What are some small changes you can make today to start taking care of your body?

8
DOES LOVING MY BODY MEAN I CAN'T CHANGE IT?

When you talk about loving yourself, accepting your imperfections, and embracing your body as it is now, it's easy to get confused about what that really means.

Some people equate accepting your body with giving up on it. Others say that if you really embrace your body, you would never want to change it in any way. Still others say that loving your body means keeping it on a strict diet and exercise regimen.

We tend to jump to extremes and try to define things

in black and white; but in reality, **loving your body is all about *degree* and *attitude*.**

Think about it in another way: let's say I don't know two words of Russian, and I'd like to learn how to speak it fluently. Does that mean I can't love myself as a person until I know how to speak Russian? Definitely not!

I can love myself as a person who doesn't speak Russian—or if I learn, as one who does. I don't let my ability to speak Russian (or lack thereof) define my self-worth.

Also, if I decide to learn Russian, I approach it in a way that enhances my life rather than detracting from it. Why? **Because I love and respect myself as a person.**

For instance, I might pursue learning the language, but I don't do it to the exclusion of other important things in my life—like eating, sleeping, working, or spending quality time with loved ones. If I sacrificed my health or my relationships in order to learn Russian, that would not be honoring my commitment to take care of myself.

I also make sure that my attitude about learning to speak Russian is a positive and realistic one. I don't sit around and think about what a scummy person I am because I don't already know Russian, and I don't think about how life isn't worth living joyfully until I know how to speak it fluently.

And if I'm trying to learn Russian, I'm patient with myself and realize I won't learn the whole language overnight. I acknowledge I have limitations as a person and can probably only learn so much in a manner of weeks or months.

Granted, learning Russian might seem like an unusual example, but the principle rings true.

This is what I mean by degree and attitude: if you want to make changes and set goals for yourself or your body, **it can be a positive thing within the right framework**. Or it can be just the opposite if you drive yourself to unhealthy extremes or approach it with a negative attitude toward yourself and your body.

KEYS TO POSITIVE CHANGE

Let's take one of the most common ways women want to change their bodies: weight loss. Again, it's all about the *attitude* you have about pursuing weight loss, and the *degree* to which you go to do it. There are some important questions that you should think about.

Why do you want to lose weight? Is it because you believe you'd be genuinely healthier at a lower weight? Or do you feel like your body is *unacceptable* and *unworthy* until you lose weight?

It's one thing to think you might feel a little more comfortable if you lose weight, it's another to think you're not "good enough" until you do.

Are you sacrificing your health in order to achieve a certain weight? Sure, the diet industry acts like health and weight loss go hand in hand, but this isn't always the case. Even if you're overweight, *weight loss isn't healthy if it comes about in a way that puts your health at risk.*

Crash diets and extremely restrictive diets completely ignore what the body needs to function on a daily basis (i.e. energy and nutrients) and make following a plan

and a number on a scale more important than listening to your body and keeping yourself healthy.

Studies demonstrate that if you're overweight, improvements in your health can be achieved through positive lifestyle changes *with or without weight loss*. That means that eating well, sleeping well, and being active in a healthy way can all improve your health, whether or not your weight changes in the process. **Aim for being truly healthy—not just reaching a number on a scale.**

Are you sacrificing your peace of mind to achieve a certain weight? In the process of focusing on weight loss, it's not uncommon to find yourself obsessed with what you eat and what you look like. Suddenly you're always thinking about calories, fat grams, or what size swimsuit you can wear. You worry that you won't be able to refuse the cake at your mom's birthday party next week, and that might mean not fitting into your "motivation" jeans (two sizes too small) in the closet.

When your efforts to lose weight start to consume every waking minute of your day, it's time to take stock of your priorities. If weight loss feels like it's taking over

your life, get some of your life back by making time for other important things like your mental well-being, your relationships, and your physical health—things that are much more important than how fast a number on the scale is going down. Be flexible with yourself and take the long-term approach instead of just focusing on short-term results.

Are your expectations realistic and sustainable? Sometimes when your physical or mental health is suffering as a result of your weight-loss efforts, your body is trying to give you a hint. If you have to maintain a restrictive diet and intense exercise routine just to get to a certain weight, it might be time to reevaluate whether your goals are realistic. This is a good time to ask yourself *why* you really want to get to this goal weight and whether or not it's the genuinely healthy thing for you to do.

These standards apply to more than just weight loss. Makeup is another good example. Spending 5-10 minutes in the morning putting on a little makeup doesn't have to be a bad thing. You might feel a little

more put together and ready to take on the world with a brush of mascara and a dab of lip gloss. But if you spend over an hour doing your makeup every day and sometimes it makes you late for work, that's a problem (*degree*). Or if you think you look hideous without makeup and that you're not worth looking at without it, that's also an issue (*attitude*).

You can use these examples for almost any other way you want to change, alter, or enhance your appearance. **It's all about the degree to which you do things and if what you're doing is adding or subtracting from your quality of life.**

Only you can make that decision, but it's important to become aware and be honest about your attitude toward your body and how it's affecting your life.

TAKE ACTION!

It's time to think about whether or not your habits concerning your appearance are healthy ones. Make a list of appearance habits you spend time on each day.

Include ones that might seem insignificant. Here are a few examples:

- Applying makeup and styling your hair.

- Retouching your makeup and hair throughout the day.

- Checking in the mirror.

- Asking others how you look or if you look okay.

- Measuring body parts, counting flaws (like pimples), etc.

- Washing your face.

- Tanning.

- Shaving or hair removal.

- Planning meals.

- Exercising.

Now, most of these things aren't a big deal, as long as they don't consume too much of your time or thoughts. Some, like planning meals and exercising, can be very healthy in the right context. For instance, checking on your appearance in the mirror isn't a bad thing, but

if you're checking every ten minutes and constantly focusing on your flaws, then that's a whole other ball of wax. Similarly, exercising can be a very healthy habit, but if you're spending so much time at the gym that your health and your personal relationships are suffering, then you need to question whether sacrificing these parts of yourself is really worth it.

Next, I want you to ask yourself two questions about each habit you listed:

1. Do you spend a reasonable or unreasonable amount of time on it?

2. Do you think this habit has a positive or negative impact in your life?

Circle the habits you feel may be excessive or have a negative impact on your life. These are the areas where you can start setting new priorities.

9
THE COMPLETE PACKAGE

- Body hate surfaces when we place *too* much importance on the way we look.

- Your appearance doesn't mean nothing, but it also doesn't mean *everything*.

- If you really want to be happy, then you have to look at yourself as a complete package.

EXPAND YOUR SENSE OF SELF

Your body and your physical features are *part* of who you are, but they're not even close to being the *whole* you–

or even the most important part of you! And the way you feel about who you are as a person needs to extend beyond what you feel about the way you look.

> *If your entire sense of self comes from the way you look, then it's safe to say you will feel defeated on days when your hair isn't looking its best, your outfit doesn't fit quite right, or your skin has a breakout. It's like the saying that you shouldn't put all your eggs in one basket—you certainly don't want your self-esteem to come from just one place. Having multiple sources of self-worth—a job you enjoy, friends and family you love, a cause that makes you feel passionate, a hobby that absorbs you, a community you invest in—will ultimately lead to a happier, healthier, more confident you.*

✳ Rosie Molinary, *Beautiful You.*

Be more than just what you look like. You are more than the color of your hair, the shape of your legs, or the circumference of your waistline. These are only some of your features. But when you think of yourself primarily in terms of how you look, then you're discounting the

rest of your unique qualities. If your appearance is your priority, then you're not allowing other aspects of yourself to develop. It's sort of like personality atrophy. When your time, energy and thoughts are wrapped up in worrying about your body, then other parts of yourself and your life are going to be neglected.

GETTING TO KNOW YOU...

So if you're not just a collection of physical features, then who are you? Getting to know yourself and learning to love yourself as a person can work wonders for how you feel about your body. After all, your body is the wonderful vessel that makes YOU possible. **But it's hard to love someone you don't even know, so take the time to get to know yourself!**

If you feel like you don't really know who you are, it's time to do a little digging. It doesn't have to be complicated, and we're not looking for sweeping labels that put your personality into a neat little box. You just want to put together all the little pieces that

make you the unique individual that you are. Ask yourself these questions:

- Do I enjoy socializing with friends, or do I prefer to spend time alone? Or do I need a little of both?

- Do I work best when I dive into a project and do it all at once? Or do I like to work in bits and pieces?

- What brings out my creativity? Is it music? Or art? Speaking to a group of people? Putting my organizational skills to use? Figuring out how things work?

- What is something I've accomplished that makes me really proud? How can I learn from that experience?

- What relationships mean the most to me in my life? What people are important to me?

- What helps me relax and unwind? A walk outside? A good novel? A sappy movie? A hot bath? Journaling? Playing guitar? Talking with friends?

- What hobbies and topics bring out my passionate side? Helping others? Politics? Gardening? Health? Can I pursue something in these areas to help me develop my passions?

Remember, there are no wrong answers here! It's just about learning who you are and coming to appreciate yourself from different angles.

When you get to know yourself as a person, you discover what makes you feel happy and fulfilled in your life, and what doesn't. Then you have a starting place where you can begin to pursue what really brings meaning to your life, while leaving behind old habits that hold you back.

THE COMPARISON BLUES

One common symptom of body hate is constant comparison. Critical thoughts about your own appearance tend to spread to how you think about others as well. After all, if you're in the habit of scrutinizing every little flaw on your own body, it's not much of a leap to start doing the same to those around you, too.

Comparing is competing. Someone has to win, and someone has to lose. She may have "better" hair, but you have "better" thighs, right? Comparing and judging are just different ways of keeping your own body hate alive and kicking. It just perpetuates the cycle of determining your self-worth (and the worth of others) by measuring imperfections and making sweeping judgments.

Now that you're getting to know yourself as a complete package, it's time to start doing the same toward others. We are all who we are, a complete and unique package of different traits and attributes. We have different strengths and weaknesses, different pasts and different futures. **Comparing means you're judging at a surface level and not looking at the big picture, instead of valuing yourself and others as complete people.**

Think of it this way: apple pie is awesome, and chocolate cake is also awesome. Different recipes, different outcomes. But the awesomeness of apple pie doesn't cancel out the awesomeness of chocolate cake

or vice versa. They can both be awesome in their own unique and individual way.

It's the same with us. **One person's unique beauty doesn't cancel out anyone else.** We all have our own beauty. Find yours and embrace it.

TAKE ACTION!

Make a list of aspects of yourself you feel could use some development, maybe areas that have been neglected during the time you've struggled with negative body thoughts.

Do you want to read more books? Learn a new language? Get in touch with your artistic side? Learn to handle stress more effectively? Start doing more volunteer work? Call an old friend and reconnect? Spend more time with your family? Learn to ski or surf or hang glide or do yoga? Go visit a local historical site? Go on a road trip across the country? Get your finances in order? Start a business?

What do you want to do? Who do you want to be?

The possibilities are truly endless, and it's all up to you. Start working on expanding your sense of self and broadening your definition of what makes you who you are. When your time, energy and thoughts are focused on other positive pursuits, then negative body thoughts lose their power over you and no longer become the center of your life.

FINAL THOUGHTS

Thank you so much for taking the time to read this book! I hope it has brought you closer to having a positive relationship with your body. Just remember, learning to love your body is a process, and it doesn't happen overnight. Take it one step at a time and enjoy the journey!

If you have any thoughts or questions about this book, please don't hesitate to visit *www.livingthenourishedlife.com* and go to the Contact page to find the best way to reach me. I look forward to hearing from you!

If you haven't already, please join me on Facebook [*facebook.com/thenourishedlife*] and Pinterest [*pinterest. com/nourishedlife1/*] if you'd like to stay in touch.

All the best,

✳ *Elizabeth*

READ MORE!

If enjoyed reading this book, you might want to check out my other eBook *The Nourished Metabolism* to learn more about how diet, stress and exercise affect your metabolism. Visit *livingthenourishedlife. com/metabolism-ebook* to learn more.

RESOURCES

RESOURCES AND REFERENCES FOR THIS BOOK INCLUDE:

Bacon L, Aphramor L. *Weight science: evaluating the evidence for a paradigm shift.* Nutr J. 2011.

Gaesser GA, Angadi SS, Sawyer BJ. *Exercise and diet, independent of weight loss, improve cardiometabolic risk profile in overweight and obese individuals.* Phys Sportsmed. 2011.

Hirschmann, Jane R. and Munter, Carol H. *When Women Stop Hating Their Bodies: Freeing Yourself from Food and Weight Obsession.* The Random House Publishing Group. 1995.

Molinary, Rose. *Beautiful You: A Daily Guide to Radical Self Acceptance.* Seal Press. 2010.

Wilhelm, Sabine. *Feeling Good About the Way You Look: A Program for Overcoming Body Image Problems.* The Guilford Press. 2006.

33011118R00063

Made in the USA
Middletown, DE
26 June 2016